Corridor

CORRIDOR

Jonathan Aaron

Wesleyan University Press

Published by University Press of New England
Hanover & London

Wesleyan University Press
Published by University Press of New England,
Hanover, NH 03755
© 1992 by Jonathan Aaron
All rights reserved
Printed in the United States of America   5 4 3 2 1
CIP data appear at the end of the book

"Below Argentina," "Your Angela," and "The Con-
sultation" previously appeared in *The Western Hu-
manities Review*; "The Last of the Medici" in *The
New Republic*; "The Voice from Paxos" in *The New
York Review of Books*; "From the 1929 Edition of
the Encyclopaedia Brittanica" in *Partisan Review*;
"Dance Mania" and "Sufficiency" in *The Paris Re-
view*; "The Heart" in *The London Review of Books*;
"The Best Years of Our Lives" in *Off The Page*;
"Turbulence" in *The Quarterly Review*.

"The Voice from Paxos" was reprinted in *The Best
American Poetry, 1991*, published by Collier Books,
Macmillan Publishing Co. "Dance Mania" was re-
printed in *The Best American Poetry, 1992*, pub-
lished by Collier Books, Macmillan Publishing Co.

My thanks to the Corporation of Yaddo for time to
finish a number of these poems.

Jekyll knows very well who
Hyde is, but the
knowledge is not reciprocal.

  —Julio Cortázar

And I thought of the door
With no lock to lock.

  —Robert Frost

Contents

Corridor

Street Music

I dreamed it was November 1930.
Walking east on the Boulevard St-Germain
toward the Odéon, just past the rue Kelver
(a cross street that in fact never existed),
in the midst of people hurrying (it was cold
and getting late), I saw a woman crouched
against a wall, bundled in a scarf and a cheap
light-blue overcoat. She held an accordion
that appeared to be made entirely of wood.
Its notes could have come from a muffled xylophone.
A glimpse of her small, half-turned-away face
showed her to be at least eighty, which meant
she'd been born around 1850, if not earlier.
I felt exempted from my whereabouts,
carried back to the middle of the previous century.
The thought of her life coming forward from then to this
particular moment in this city in this dream
I knew I was dreaming was like a pool of water
I wanted to reach into for what glittered there.
But I couldn't stop to give her a coin—the money
in my pocket hadn't been invented yet.

The Heart

I woke up to your knocking,
convinced someone was patrolling the corridor,
hammering the doors.
The heat was intense, and I wished it would rain.
Your name came to me,
and I thought about all I'd once known about you
but forgot, and once again I saw
those glossy textbook illustrations
full of bright colors, capital letters, Latin names,
those likenesses that used to take my breath away in school.
And then I began to recall more—
the Greeks thought your purpose was to cool
the quick temper of the blood,
and it took the lucid Harvey boatloads of snakes
and apes and other farfetched creatures
to bring your secret to light.
Now I'm standing at the window,
noting the haze, the faintness of the stars,
but thinking of you, little fist
clenching and unclenching as if determined
to keep at it forever,
snug as a treasure carefully packed for shipment
to a distant museum. And I think of Byron
staring into the flames near the water's edge,
and of what he wrote afterward to Moore, ". . . all
of Shelley was consumed but for the *heart*."
Wherever you are—
in the open chest of the accusatory martyr
who leaned toward me one day in an Italian church,
or on the sleeves of the young, the madly
hopeful and in love—you do what you must,
solitary stoker down there in the body's hold,
bending to your labor
inspired, certain of yourself. Pure and blind.

The Children's Crusade

Next comes a little town
with a First Congregational Church
and a restaurant called The Lobster Pit.
We're thirsty after so many countries.
I drink a glass of water and try to remember
where we started from and think about
how when you forget something
it means your brain cells are dying.
A waiter brings us food in the parking lot.
I eat some fried clams and stand on my head.
I know there's such a thing as smart food—
nobody has to tell me Nature has her ways.
Today the countryside flew past our bus so fast
I couldn't count the crows on snow or the cows
lining up for their barns or the kids
playing hockey with sticks and stones
on little lakes that kept changing shape
even though each one was frozen.
But so what? Winter doesn't mean much
when it comes to the way things look at you
funny when you look at them. Any season,
it's the same world, squiggly lines and shapes
that become tall puddles when you're close enough
to see how they shine, all fuzzy and worn-out
at the edges—houses, trees, clouds leaning toward us
with friendly expressions, wanting us to wait,
but falling behind, getting smaller and smaller,
like everybody who said, You're safer with us, don't go.
But we did, and it was like waking up
and finding my best dream staying with me
in a completely new kind of waking up,
telling me, "Well, now I'm going to be your real life."

3

Below Argentina

What language barrier? We got along famously,
monitoring the astronomical and geographical
stations any map shows huddled in twos and threes
near the blue toes of the glacier. The days passed quickly,
but not the nights peculiar to that latitude.
The fire in an oil drum heaving sparks and ash
in crazy patterns skyward. The heavens so cold
we could hear the stars ringing like neglected telephones.
We fenced diplomatically over my country's
traditional concern for underwater monsters, snowmen and astrology,
but I couldn't stop imagining her inside all that goose down.
She warned me absentmindedness leads to property damage,
personality breakdown. It's out of our hands,
I explained. More than politics has thrown us together
on this godforsaken piece of volcanic pastry.
But appearances sometimes take on lives of their own,
and suddenly I no longer knew how to stand in their way:
Whatever was happening had already started.
We were facing each other on a coastal abutment
opposite some evil-looking rocks called the Sewing Machine Needles.
Heedless of the wind she unzipped her anorak.
I glimpsed the wire beneath her left breast
just before we kissed in a white glare
like a movie screen's when the film is about to start.

"The Best Years of Our Lives"

—for Bill Corbett

Toward the end of the movie Harold Russell, back from the war,
is standing in his parents' darkened kitchen. Just before
he sees Cathy O'Donnell on the other side of the screen door
he picks up a bottle of milk with his steel hook to pour
himself a glass. What happens next is a love scene,
but I keep seeing that milk bottle, which glows
as if lit from within. How its shoulders taper
to a neck thin enough so that even as a kid I could
pour the heavy cream at the top into a pitcher.
How I pried with my thumbnail the paper
bottle cap's slightly off-center tab. How,
after the briefest use, the tab tore and the cap
wore out, frayed to an abject, scuffed transparency.

Tales of Good and Evil

The outskirts of the city flickered
in the darkening train compartment.
A bell passed, ringing
like a spoon dropped down a stairwell.
I gave up trying to read

the dog-eared *Tales of Good and Evil*
the hotel clerk had tossed me
with a laugh as the authorities
were leading me off to the station.
A porter came and went, pouring

re-reheated tea. North became another
hemisphere, another time of year.
Drowsy, I returned to the courtroom's
fluorescent chill, the frog
in the throat of the public-address system.

Or saw more smoke and the same
high-fashion agitator, her black dress
ripped, her revolutionary cheekbones
hollow in the glare of the trouble
she'd started. My fire hazard, I told her,

my beautiful false move, and I'd wake up
to barer scenery, even hotter sun.
Nobody asked for my papers when I arrived.
The occasional lounging policeman
cradled an M-16, but behind his sunglasses

he was anybody's guess. The plaza's
torpid façades shimmered and tipped,

a handful of palm trees naturally casting
no shade. I was checking my repertoire
of cheap attention-getting devices

when a fan belt sang and a taxi
caught up with me, its dashboard
madonna on fire under beads and fringe.
She told me I'd come to my senses
here on the porch of the Casa Marina,

a bottle beside me, a glass in my hand.
And the sea rubs a pale strip of beach
like someone patiently honing a knife.
A little wind carries talk from a nearby
dirt-floor café, elbows the lantern

hung dimly over my head. I'm staring
in the direction of the oil refinery,
checking my watch, waiting for the flash
and the report, the secondary detonations,
and the sky to unclose all at once and show me

the real one hiding behind it. The moment comes
for holding my breath. No wonder
a siren starts to whine in the distance.
No wonder the neighborhood dogs already sound like
children up past their bedtime practicing hymns.

Your Angela

—for J. B.

I'm out for an evening stroll near the reservoir
whacking a few vague ferns with my new cane,
when the past, a surreptitious, cumulative presence,
comes up to me and offers freedom
from the statistics I count on—the telephone numbers,
the transportation and hotel expenses, the rates of exchange.
"Remember something you wanted that didn't happen?
Times have changed since yesterday. It can."
I wonder if I should start an argument. But I'm no different
from anybody else, just an ordinary mobile zone
of molecular spasm and habit. Besides, there's a touch of the sea
in the darkening air, of the flower-scented, the palpable
dream, and I know it's no bright ship approaching
over the water, but a slow parade of glowing dioramas.
Scene after scene floats by in luminous succession
as if offered on a stadium-sized lazy Susan, each
a picture window framing a missed opportunity, a botched
accomplishment, each inviting me to the ceremony of its
restoration, and my own. In one bright panel a train
is moving south through valleys of olive trees to an island
I never arrived at. In another, a man I never met
sits in a café wondering why the statues he's famous for
keep getting smaller and smaller. In another, the Pacific
I never saw from the crest of a high dune flashes its million bulbs
at a rising moon. Now an old landscape shimmers into view
and steadies itself for me to contemplate—
more trees, a tall brick house they partially obscure,
some passing clouds, the echoes of a bell
striking the hour. I make my choice, turning onto
the road leading in. No one is following as I shift
into second and reposition my hands on the cracked,
discolored plastic steering wheel. The tires are silent
on the pale asphalt, like the windshield wipers

when the rain begins, like the old Dodge itself finally gliding
to a stop by the verandah steps. Then come the sound effects
of the situation, the definitive *thunk* of the car door
closing, the footsteps of the wordless girl
who leads me along an upstairs hall, the draft hissing through
the open window once she leaves me to unpack my things.
I notice a book lying open on the bedside table.
As I reach for it a sudden, high-pitched gust tears
at the pages, but when I pick it up and examine it by lamplight
I know what I'm looking for: this cartoon of a woman's face
beneath an arrangement of stars and these words slanting downward
on the inside cover: *My Darling George, At Last, Your Angela—*

The Consultation

I'd sense someone rushing from the room, but never
turned quickly enough to see more than a furtive, headlong
scuttle, the birdlike flapping of an oversized
dinner jacket. Wondering if there was a medical
term for this experience, I decided to visit M.,
long noted for brilliance in the field of behavioral research.
At first he seemed distracted by the ebb
and flow of the badminton tournament taking place
on the impeccable green below the terrace where,
weather permitting, he liked to conduct his interviews.
Harried cameramen were fussing with grips and tripods,
skirmishers in the ceaseless war of nerves
doctors of this sort feel compelled to wage
for experimental purposes. Are you very
superstitious? he asked. We were drinking coffee.
I glanced at my cup, noting its guileless folk design—
upside-down-looking elephants painted rightside-up—
as sounds of the match in progress echoed bravely,
lulling, ancestral. The players could have been
survivors of the Tsar's home movies. A shuttlecock
dropped at our feet and instantly expired. M. continued
turning the pages of a *National Geographic*.
Whenever I look in a mirror I can't see my eyes move.
I suspect certain automobiles have second thoughts.
Words like gland and autopsy label my fate.
So how can I explain I wasn't surprised
by the squall bearing down on us? The edge of the lake
was operating at a low boil. Farther out,
sailboats at their moorings reared and plunged
like spooked horses. Suddenly he slapped his knee.
Malocchio! he declared, the evil eye,
and beckoned me back inside. As the door closed behind us
rain hit the terrace with a noise like coal down a chute.

The Varus Problem

Quintilius Varus, Commander of the Northern Army,
"a man of luxurious habits, disturbed
by no cares," refuses to listen to veteran observers
and leads over fifteen thousand regular troops
into the Teutoberger Wald, an offshoot
of the great Hercynian forest, planning to make
an example of what he takes for a minor tribal
uprising. On the third day of an immense rain
Arminius, a young native chieftain in imperial employ,
watches the ponderous column of armor
bog down in finally impassable pine and brier.
When the moment stares him in the face
he gives the signal, and German hordes
break in on the Romans from all sides.

A disaster of classic proportions,
marked by fiery night skies all over Italy,
it prevents the latinization of much of today's
western Germany. Some historians assert it denies
the peoples of the north a high culture
and prompts them to sweep south with a low one.
Some dwell on logistics and the fullness of time.
The Emperor Augustus wept when he heard the news.
Rome must have offended Jupiter, he said,
and promised games in honor of the god
as soon as the military situation had improved.
But from then on he was given
to leaning his head against a wall and crying,
"Quintilius Varus, give me back my legions!"

Sufficiency

Dozens of burning, fish-shaped clouds dove for the horizon,
determined to make more of an already explosive sunset.

The sea gave the shore another hearty slap on the back.
Crickets started singing in the dry grass beyond the wide-open door.

The day's last excursion boat glided past the window, white as a gull.
We were about to sit down around the kitchen table

and serve ourselves from a hot bowl those little red potatoes
the whole island survived on during the war.

Bréhat

Still Life Beside a Lake

(after Vladimír Holan)

Yes, everything's here, everything's right
where it should be, tranquil, luminous, sublime.
The wisdom of the ages, bread and books.
Not a hair on the nib of your pen;
you won't have to wipe it on your sleeve.
And you can be sure the wine cellar harbors only wine.
The elements present themselves—wind, stars, a storm.
But you're already dreaming up the names of sailing ships,
can't wait to get out of this place . . .

Before you can say them aloud, or even sooner,
you're going to be running for your life,
like the pilgrim who fled Olympus because
he couldn't find a single goddess there.

The Last of the Medici

Cosimo III adds to his relic collection
a piece of the intestine of St. Francis Xavier,
leaving politics to his sons, first Ferdinando,
already wandering in syphilitic amnesia,
then Gian Gastone, who hires the penniless
to copulate in front of his dinner guests.

Meanwhile, defenseless, swept by the plague,
Florence continues falling to pieces
cornice by cornice, its piazzas empty
and flyblown by the time the Austrians
take over with fewer than 6,000 troops.

They concede an apartment in the Pitti Palace
to Anna Maria, the Electress Palatine,
childless, the end of the line. Standing immobile
and furious beneath a black canopy in a room
crammed with her family's silver furniture,
she receives a few visitors, including
the English poet Thomas Gray, but refuses
medical advice, unwilling to contemplate dying.

In February 1743, her physicians deliver
a message that the end is near.
Much older than her 75 years, she's given last rites
as a hurricane flogs the broken back of the city.
Afterward the story spreads that the wind
snatched her up like a leaf and carried her off.

An Interruption

"It's you," he says, extending an arm
from the spiky shadows of a privet hedge.
I catch a quick, reproachful glint off his glasses,
but I'm not surprised. The park is crawling
with such apparitions—they rummage in the greenery,
aberrant and lost, sifting the remains
of private histories, armed with an ax to grind
or a bone to pick. This one's already
telling me about his wife's motel
weekends with his accountant, amnesia following
the discovery of their shallow graves
in a wildlife sanctuary, the legal subterfuge
that landed him here, stripped of everything
. and announcing to a perfect stranger, *"This"*—
he brandishes a manila envelope—
"contains my reconstruction of what
exactly happened on the night it did.
Consider," he says,
"how life goes on without us
all the time—footprints in the snow,
the calm of a solitary hour, intelligent dust.
What could be simpler than perusing
a few highlights of the evidence on my behalf?"
A window shade rolls up with a sudden bang.
In the cavernous lobby of the old Savoy
he's lunging for the elevator as the police
close in. Or apologizing on the witness stand,
wiping his forehead with a handkerchief.
Or running the light in that purple Cadillac
just as I launch myself from the curb.
He suggests we talk business at a steak house "where
they really know how to handle a piece of meat."
I remember the place, its fake-French maître d',

the aggressive torpor of its waitresses,
a doorless phone booth. And for a moment
I glimpse my future as someone else
in another part of the world,
someone with a different past, a man who
never stood here listening, suddenly alert
to the sights and sounds of his surroundings—
the office buildings soaring into darkness,
the pointless traffic just beyond the trees
like the ocean, or the breath of anyone
sinking into sleep as the night deepens
and the wind, sorting its messages, moans a little.

Cigarettes

1.

The girl on the station platform who asked me
breathlessly for a light reeked of tobacco,
but who was I to tell her she was harming herself?
"Two packs a day for forty years," the defiant formula
of the bride's grandfather at a recent wedding.
His gold lighter and his cuff links matched.
I could see myself in his Porsche sunglasses.
In the Sears parking lot, a large, unshaven man sat with his dog
in the front seat of a white Continental, windows up,
engine running for the air conditioner.
As I passed he brought a burning match close to his nose.
He looked like someone trying hard to read a thermometer.

2.

Creatures of habit, they're in something like limbo now,
projections of the forlorn cheer an occasional billboard
proposes, exiles from a stillness
that's pure in the medium of Steichen
or Capa, but not in mine, since
I can't go a day without recalling
the intimate heft of a fresh, unbroken pack
in my shirt pocket—that gently obtrusive firmness
marking my heart—and how it felt to wonder, with a mild
but increasing agitation, what would prompt me this time
to produce it with a special deftness
always of the wrist, to pull at the little red belt,
lift the cellophane, tear at the foil . . .

3.

It had to be the experience of uncertainty,
a resonance of my inability to visualize
what I looked like, know where I was. Any chance

reflection brought a surprise. But the purposeful
flare of the match released a knowing
calm that remained as the effects rushed in, spreading
a message to the farthest reaches of my lungs.
Veiled in a blue cloud that came and went, rose, drifted
or flew according to the scenario my gestures roused,
I could feel my eyes grow narrow ("steely"). I walked
more slowly, each stride covered more ground
because I was taller now ("rangy"). Canny generosity
transformed my approach to anyone I met.
I became ready for anything, and my name, compressed
to a single syllable ("Vince" or "Tod"),
was as outright and unarguable as a punch in the jaw.

4.

I see myself hunched over a leaf of flame,
cupping my hands as if to protect it from the storm
or myself from a sniper's eye. I'm serious,
in an acrid haze. Now F. appears
in a blur not entirely caused by snow, or dusk,
or the passage of years. Leaning closer,
trying to see each other better, we're both peering
with determination through thickening silver eddies.
How wonderful it is doing this, feeling important
and sharing the same brand! Then T., inhaling
with a hiss and a significant glance.
And L., groping for her scissors in a slow,
depressive turbulence of ash. And W.,
demanding silence for The Moonwalk, fist to her mouth,
her whole body tensing for that cough she endowed
with the authority of a biblical text.

5.

I used to like a martini on the rocks with a lemon
twist—a drink, I felt, that always did what you wanted.
Alone or not, an hour or so before dinner
I'd scrupulously set forth the stocky fifth of gin,

the green and sidelong bottle of vermouth,
a bucket of ice, a book of matches, and an unbroken
pack of the latest I'd turned to. It was crucial
that the pack be new. Its freshness, not the drink's,
gave promise to the evening's prospects.
As the sun went down and the woods intensified
beyond the window, coalescing, it often seemed, to a single
branch whose clicks and squeaks sounded ever more
deliberate, and as the day's unfinished business
slyly and vengefully gained weight on my desk

6.
(those stacks of papers and books that rose toward the ceiling
at a rate past my control), I could believe
there was time enough before sleep for discovery
and recuperation. I'd watch the ice cubes test
the surface of the gin, their efforts not to melt into the tidal
swirls of alcohol meandering at mid-level in the glass.
But I'd ponder the plumes unraveling from my hand,
those azure filaments weaving toward the upper shadows
where, I imagined, the unborn minutes were lining up
like little sky divers, eager to leap. And, my thoughts hovering
on the edge of arrival, I must have neared a sort of faith
that somehow, after all, I could mark what would happen,
make it mine as it fell into the act of taking place.

7.
I don't know how long I stood at the window
watching the enormous chestnut tree across the road,
its vast, brain-shaped cupola tossing and flashing
as if to thoughts it couldn't shake off.
Whatever I noticed had something on its mind.
The window darkened, the tree went away for the night.
The cat retreated from herself as my own shape
shifted from thin to fat and back to thin
in the lights of cars slowing down for a hairpin turn.
A truck changing gears was someone trying to speak.

The black **X** I'd imposed on the day-in-question's
empty little square stood out on the kitchen calendar,
two lines signaling cancellation, I wasn't sure of what.
Light-headed, I combed the house again, believing
the whisper of any shadowy niche I could trick myself
into thinking I'd missed before. My luck amounted
to a few shreds of nearly odorless tobacco
in the pocket of a coat I hadn't worn since spring.
Looking at those particles in my palm,
wondering if eating them would be worth it,
I suspected I'd arrived at the edge of the known world.

8.
Some mornings I can see so clearly
I'm certain I'm still asleep. Such sounds—
a lot of delicate, shivery violins,
Monteverdi or Mantovani, it depends.
Such texture and color—heavy woolens
and the purple of a plum. Where, I ask,
did the blue of that sky come from? The empty cloud
overhead just waiting for words and punctuation?
The light in the trees taking its time to brighten
or fade, it hardly matters which? And then
I catch a whiff of contradiction—a touch, perhaps
of the old-time ritual of burning leaves,
or of the city's unadulterated diesel air.
What keeps on happening comes back, and I see
my own afterimage on the bed, faintly aglow
as it dissolves in the air I've stirred by waking up.
And in the hours that pass, any gesture—
dialing a number, ordering a beer,
consulting an atlas for someplace far away to get to—
leaves a gauzy imprint on the space
surrounding me, a sign so slight
that my noticing it results in its erasure.

9.

And then it occurs to me that the logic of my condition
might actually lead somewhere beyond its consequences.
To a seacoast in a different climate, say,
a cliff rising from the ocean's nervous coils,
a terrace daringly suspended over brightness.
Looking down to the left through a stand of cypresses
I see the gleam of marble columns, prone, in pieces,
bones of a civilization I'm returning to at last.
Summer is over, the hotel is nearly empty.
On the table before me a cup on a saucer
gives off a momentary wisp of steam.
Next to it, a shot glass of whatever I asked the waiter
to surprise me with, and a folded newspaper,
weeks out of date, I haven't got around to reading yet.
Next to that, the pack of cigarettes
from which I pry a single, pure example. Striking a match,
I'm overwhelmed by my view of the islands.

Turbulence

Suddenly the girl in front of me springs to her feet,
white-faced, hand to her mouth, desperate for proof
she's about to wake up from this dream
we're all falling into, this dream full of thumps
and shudders as the air darkens for the movie—
an Italian Western, its opening shot of mesas and desert
invaded by a tangle of hair or dust twisting slowly
upward, an almost intelligible scribble.

Glancing out my window one more time
before pulling the shade, I see the little silver
blade of the wing rising and falling, a gesture
I used to connect with feathers and migration.
A stewardess stumbles toward me with raised eyebrows.
I finger my armrest for the audio.

Dance Mania

In 1027, not far from Bernburg,
eighteen peasants were seized
by a common delusion.
Holding hands, they circled for hours
in a churchyard, haunted by visions,
spirits whose names they called in terror or welcome,
until an angry priest cast a spell on them
for disrupting his Christmas service,
and they sank into the frozen earth
up to their knees. In 1227
on a road to Darmstadt, scores of children
danced and jumped in a shared delirium.
Some saw devils, others the Savior enthroned
in the open heavens. Those who survived
remained palsied for the rest of their days.
And in 1278, two hundred fanatics raved on a bridge
that spanned the Mosel near Koblenz.
A cleric passed carrying the host
to a devout parishioner, the bridge collapsed,
and the maniacs were swept away.
A hundred years later, in concert with
the Great Mortality, armies of dancers
roved in contortions all over Europe.
The clergy found them immune to exorcism,
gave in to their wishes and issued
decrees banning all but square-toed shoes,
the zealots having declared they hated
pointed ones. They disliked even more
the color red, suggesting
a connection between their malady
and the condition of certain infuriated
animals. Most of all they could not endure
the sight of people weeping.

The Swiss doctor Paracelsus was the first to call
the Church's theories of enchantment
nonsensical gossip. Human life is inseparable
from the life of the universe, he said.
Anybody's mortal clay is an extract
of all beings previously created. Illness
can be traced, he said,
to the failure of the Archaeus, a force
residing in the stomach and whose function
is to harmonize the mystic elements (salt,
sulphur, mercury) on which vitality depends.
He advocated direct measures, proposed remedies
fitting the degree of the affliction.
A patient could make a wax doll of himself,
invest his sins and blasphemies within the manikin,
then burn it with no further ceremony.
He could subject himself to ice-water baths,
or submit to starvation in solitary confinement.
Noted for his arrogance, vanity
and choler (his real name was Theophrastus Bombast
von Hohenheim), Paracelsus made enemies.
They discovered he held no academic degree
and caused him to be banished from Basle,
to become a wanderer who would die mysteriously
at the White Horse Inn in Salzburg in 1541.
After a drunken orgy, said one report.
The victim of thugs hired by jealous apothecaries,
said another. And the dance mania
found its own way through time to survive
among us, as untouched as ever by the wisdom of science.
Think of the strange, magnetic sleep
whole populations fall into every day,
in gymnasiums full of pounding darkness,
in the ballrooms of exclusive hotels,
on verandahs overlooking the ocean and played upon
by moonlight, in backyards, on the perfect lawns

of great estates, on city rooftops, in any brief field
the passing tourist sees as empty—
how many millions of us now, the living
and the dead, hand in hand as always,
approaching the brink of the millennium.

Waking and Sleeping

—for Peter Hughes

He hasn't quite finished his book
about the 16th-century Anabaptist
Bockelson, who called himself
King of the New Jerusalem
and took the entire city of Münster with him
straight to hell,
but in May 1936,
Fritz Reck-Malleczewen, aged 51,
starts another. In it,
far from inquiring into the past,
he's going to describe what it's like
being present at the end of the world.
In a 600-year-old farmhouse by a lake east of Munich,
he writes at night,
then hides the results—
each entry is a capital offense—
sometimes out in the barn,
sometimes in a hole in the ground
among the pine trees.
He mourns Spengler, abandoned by history,
wrecked by the huge dinners and vintage wines
the Ruhr businessmen he'd given in to and loathed
supplied him with. Remembers
Hitler, circa 1920, seedy party-crasher
perched on the edge of a chair, preaching on and on
to listeners too polite to throw him out.
Now, in the hour of Germany's *gigantic fetishism,*
as the world breaks down,
he cultivates his hatred, *waking and sleeping,*
with a kind of ardor.
The Anschluss, Kristallnacht, the fall of Poland, France—
he calls these events *beyond history.*

And smaller, briefer details: Emil Jannings
fretting about his art collection
and the continued availability of good sausage,
the suicide of Unity Mitford, would-be
Queen of Germany,
moviegoers cheering the latest
footage from the fronts.
He talks directly to his future reader,
whose existence he wants to believe in
but can't imagine.
Do you know anything, really,
about the blackness
in which we live?

*

Often months go by
before he can dig up his book,
write in it, and bury it again.
In January 1942, walking in the woods,
the cold paralyzing, he finds a fawn
mangled by dogs, tries to save it,
can't, and the sight comes back to him
of whale-killing in the South Atlantic,
the laughing harpooner loving his work.
The fact is we are dealing here with pestilence.
In Russia the Wehrmacht founders
in *a demon-world which has not, despite everything,*
let go of its gods.
From a hotel window in a small town he watches
the first bombing of Munich,
the sky to the north a curtain of fire.
He hears rumors of a *fantastic atom bomb*—just three,
it's said, will sink England like Atlantis.
He recalls a medical-school anatomy class,
the filthy attendant *brandishing his fatty knife.*

Mass madness obsesses him.
He decides Germany is a *termite heap*
and plans a postwar study:
The End of the Termites.
His house is haunted by the ghost of a monk,
sounds of heavy objects being rolled or dragged.
In a country railroad station packed with refugees
a woman drops her suitcase, clothes fall out,
a manicure kit, a toy,
and the charred corpse of a child
shrunk to the proportions of a mummy.

*

The July plotters are rounded up.
Ah, now, really, gentlemen—he addresses them
as a Prussian to Prussians—*this is a little late*
and curses them, hating them
for having played along with *godlessness*
and soullessness for as long as they did.
On a hot day, on a bus, he sees a teenage girl
slap an old man slow getting on. Twice,
across the face, *I returned the compliment.*
He suffers from angina.
He gets word his son is a prisoner of the Russians.
Arrests, and more arrests. He suspects he's doomed
like everyone else. In October
1944, in a cell
four feet wide by six feet long, headed,
though he doesn't know it, for Dachau,
he manages to make some last notations,
pondering something strange—
the vanishing of his desire for revenge.
A memory occurs to him: Years earlier
he beat half to death
an *old friend* whom he'd helped and who then
took to *undermining my marriage.*

28

None of it, he saw soon afterward,
would weigh greatly
in the scales of eternity.
And then another: It's 1912,
he's aboard an English coastal steamer,
taking an evening walk on deck
with the ship's only other passenger,
a venerable professor of Asiatic religions
from Tsingtao who,
listening to the young man discourse
on Christianity's uncertain fate, turns
and looks at him for a moment,
sympathetic, understanding, and amused.

Julio Cortázar

Walking down a long corridor
on the sixth floor of the Metropole,
I turned for another backward look
and saw where I'd come from brighten
to a zone of incandescence at the vanishing point.
As I hung on this trick of perspective
a door in the middle distance opened
and there you stood,
in jeans and a white shirt rolled up at the sleeves,
feet bare, one hand on the doorknob,
the other holding your shoes.
You looked thinner than in the photographs
I instantly remembered,
but your height, untrimmed hair, beard,
and wide-apart, roundly determined eyes
were the same as ever.
You stooped and put your shoes down
carefully—placing them in the right position
just outside your door
looked like a matter of principle—straightened up,
glanced toward me and gave an offhand wave.
Then, eyebrows raised, quizzical,
you made a circular motion with a downward-pointing finger,
as if stirring an imaginary drink.
You were speaking, but your words failed to carry
above the steady hiss of the ventilation system.
Over my shoulder I saw no one
on the plush, deserted path into the next quarter hour.
Yes, *you*, you nodded,
but when I stepped toward you
you shook your head, warning me off.
Off balance, suddenly at sea,
all I could offer was the invisible object of my regret.

You shrugged and did the same, bowing slightly
as if to convey the sympathy someone who knows
might feel for someone who hasn't a clue.
It came to me it really must have been you
one rush hour years ago
in an angle of the rue du Four,
tallest among the passersby
whose reflections wavered in darkened plate-glass
like camouflage.
But how clearly I saw you now,
no longer looking in my direction, but lingering
to listen to faint applause
from a television set—or was it the rain?—
the meow of a cat becoming a baby's cry,
and footsteps hurrying out of nowhere.
Who would have thought you were about to fly away
on that special airplane of yours,
the one like a streetcar with wings,
and never come back?

From the 1929 Edition of the Encyclopaedia Britannica

—for Adam Zagajewski

The Himalayas are unclimbed,
politely marveled at.

A smiling technician poses
in the jaws of an electric generator.

A hearty account, with diagrams,
of the types of decisive attack
favored by Alexander the Great.

A short entry on Lithuania
("an independent European republic"),
the Japanese tea ceremony in twenty-seven plates,
and "a nomad fakir of India"
reading his prayers on a bed of nails.

In the Krupp works in Essen the freshly cast
steel frame of a large riveter
hangs from the ceiling
like an industrial version of Rembrandt's
"Flayed Ox."

Mussolini is "an Italian statesman" with
"obvious honesty of purpose."

A trained eagle gathers to land
on the fist of a man wearing a fencing mask,
a horsehide glove, and a double
leather sleeve for his left arm.

Recalling the Huns

We knew they were coming, the people
who lived on the shores of the Frozen Ocean,
a race, according to ancient records,
savage beyond parallel. Word reached us
they'd crossed the Volga, driving the Alani
before them, whom our government then allowed to settle
in great numbers in the northern district,
where, in poverty and exhaustion, they wondered
what they were guilty of that deserved such punishment.
Refugees began arriving with starker reports.
At birth the cheeks of the Huns are scarred by an iron,
causing hairlessness, which they take as a sign of beauty.
The Huns have no need of fire or shelter and disdain
well-flavored food, preferring to feed
on herbs and tubers such as they find on the plains,
or on the half-raw flesh of any animal,
which they warm against the backs of their horses
as they journey onward. And no longer from hearsay,
but from firsthand accounts, we learned of
their fondness for surprising their enemies,
their willfulness in negotiation, their contempt
for the gods, their unbridled love of gold.
And we knew we lay directly in the path
of their advance. What could we do,
given the speed and force of their onset,
their tirelessness in pursuit? How could we expect mercy
if not one among them could tell where he was born,
having been conceived and raised as if on the waves of a torrent,
carried along in a storm over unheard-of distances?
Then came the morning I saw twelve of them
at the eastern edge of this very field.
Clearly outlined against the arrival of fair weather,
they seemed to have risen up out of the earth, small

on their stocky mounts, smaller than I could have imagined,
some carrying lances, some those terrible bows,
a little wind stirring the feathers of their helmets.
I knew they'd seen me—how could they not have?
They made no sound as they drew together to confer
and study the four directions, looking—grouped in
silhouette—like one of those many-legged, many-minded
creatures we remember from the tales of our ancestors.

Man Ray's Photo-Portrait of
Luis Buñuel (1929)

—for David

The way that heavy face
looks out at you,
you'd take him for a young
plutocrat on his way up
in the Ministry of Mines or Railroads,
a man already banking on
a well-fed later life.
But you'd be wrong.

As he aged
he shrank to a honed, sardonic ruefulness
in an oversized sports jacket
and thick-lensed glasses.
He rarely found solid backing
for his work, lived in exile
for much of forty years, took odd jobs
in Paris, New York, and Hollywood,
found a kind of home, finally, in Mexico.
For a long time
he wasn't sure what he wanted.

Return his gaze. As you do so,
cover his right eye (the one on your left)
with a fingertip.
See how he turns into somebody
clearly determined to read
and regulate your most secret thoughts.
And that intense, slightly bug-eyed concentration
tells you you can believe him
when he says that in his student days
just by thinking about it

35

he could make girls drop to the floor
in cataleptic slumber.
Uncover the eye, now cover
the other.
Suddenly he looks a little weary,
as if he's already heard and seen enough
and wants to get out of here.

His stare, at odds with itself,
gives him away.
It shows what moved him
and the nature of his art.
Though of course that day in Man Ray's studio
his concerns were
his recurrent nightmares about money,
the erotic subterfuges of the Virgin,
the public's growing inability
to be really scandalized.

So his face is a prophecy,
as, for that matter,
whose isn't?
Go ahead—look at the photo on your
driver's license. Or proceed
to the nearest mirror.
Cover one eye, look hard, and see what you see.
Uncover the eye, now cover the other.
And as you ponder the two countries of yourself,
what you want and what you least expect,
who you are and who you well may be,

remember Luis Buñuel,
whose genius lay beyond the much he knew,
a man of simple, vehement goodwill,
aficionado of spiders, cold weather, and the dry martini,
intractable atheist
whose films are filled with angels,

to whom death was an annoying interruption,
and who, though he joked about love,
took seriously
the impossibility of satisfying
a simple desire.

The Voice from Paxos

Early in the first century, toward the end
of the increasingly destructive reign of Tiberius,
a ship was making its way slowly up
the western coast of Greece for Italy.
Having just finished supper, many of the passengers
were strolling around on deck, enjoying
another cup of wine, admiring the sunset
or the dark shoulders of Paxos, a small island of olive groves
that for a brief time separated the vessel
from the forbidding limestone headlands of Epirus.
The wind lessened, then ceased altogether.
The ship drifted. The trees near the shoreline
grew larger as they disappeared.
Suddenly a voice erupted from them calling
the name of the Egyptian helmsman, unknown to all
but a few on board. "Thamus!" it shouted, and again,
"Thamus!" When it called a third time Thamus answered,
and the voice, louder still, as if in pain
or anger, no one afterward could figure out, now said,
"When you pass near Palodes let them know
the great god Pan is dead!"
Passengers and crew alike, puzzled
or suspicious, started arguing
about the significance of what they'd just heard,
some sure the voice should be obeyed,
some certain it was crazy to get involved
in what was clearly none of their business.
If he had a good wind, Thamus decided,
he's sail past Palodes as usual,
but if he were becalmed, as they'd been a few minutes earlier,
he'd do the voice's bidding. Next morning
off Palodes, the sea was a breathless mirror.
He stepped to the rail, leaned out, and repeated the words exactly.

There was a rush of wind, and from the hazy coastline
came the sound of countless people crying out—
the sound a crowd makes when an acrobat slips fatally
from her partner's grasp, the sound of any multitude
unable to escape what it must recognize.

The Sighting

Maybe half a mile offshore the surface darkening
as if to a gust of wind, then five or six
elongated coils moving in single file
right to left, glistening, clearly *there*, as she
squints into the low afternoon sun, shading her eyes,
feeling her heart rise to the occasion, wondering
if she's actually been singled out and chosen
to see in the next instant a face rising
from the lake's million dents, perhaps that of a dog
with little winglike ears, the face she noticed once
in a granite panorama above the portals
of a French cathedral, the saved going this way,
everyone else going that, but here
and now looking around, its gaze fiery with perception,
scanning the waters, the shoreline farther off
and the bluffs above, not failing to recognize
the human figure there whose very immobility
prompts the impulse to turn toward it and investigate—

while she keeps asking it to pause
in its actual, unresponsive progress, not sure she wants
anything (a sound she's never heard, hoarse clanging
like bells and static?), but willing to settle for
the slightest sign from whatever it is
as it continues leftward, more and more out of her hands,
like yesterday or merely a minute ago, a few recursive glints
in its wake suggesting the presence of a real
unknown creature, but one so involved
in the element of its unconcern that when she looks again
she sees nothing but the lake's final, momentary
smithereens as the sun vanishes, her sighting
already something other than what meets the eye,

restored to those shadowy canyons where green
disappears into the depths of night, the first stars
becoming distinct, and the stillness around her
no longer listening as she closes her eyes
for one more wordless attempt at calling it back.

Serial Nocturne

—for Anthony Hecht

I walked long and hard, succeeding, as I
usually did, in forgetting where I was . . .

A young man returns to the city after a day
in the country. Instead of heading for
his rented room he wanders over the small bridges
spanning the small canals, and under the arches
of half-repaired marketplaces. He walks for hours.
Evening comes, then night. *Restaurant, Esso,*
Pharmacy, Bar—the neon signs go out. Good night,
see you tomorrow, people call. A fog comes in.
Ships in the harbor begin warning each other.
A clock strikes twelve. The watery pavement gleams.
Vague figures move in the shadows, cross and recross
the little square, the little bridge he's come to know.
He sees a woman standing on the bridge.
A girl. He hears her weeping. The café nearby
is closing. Two punks on a motorbike tease her,
try grabbing her purse. The young man chases them away.
She thanks him, her smile uncertain. He walks her home.
Her clothes are threadbare, she's not glamorous,
but her sadness warms him, draws him on. She agrees
to meet him on the bridge at ten o'clock
tomorrow night. When the time comes she runs
from him, terrified. Then she calms down, relents
and, once more on the bridge, tells him her story:
Her father, then her mother disappeared.
She lives with her grandmother and aunt.
The three of them mend tapestries and rugs.
All but blind, her grandmother pins her grand-
daughter's dress to hers to keep her close.
One day a man arrived to rent a room,
a handsome man, imposing, serious.
He didn't say much, kept mostly to himself.

Later, when he was out, she went up to his room.
She put her nose to each of the jars and bottles
on the dresser, looked at herself in the mirror
on whose frame his black hat hung.
She was examining a stack of well-thumbed paperbacks
when the door opened. Do you like to read? he asked.
He gave her the books and suggested she have dinner
with him at a place he knew. She shook her head.
Do you plan to spend the rest of your life—
he made a sweeping gesture with his hand—like this?
The old ladies insisted she read to them from the books,
which were murder mysteries, violent, graphic
("Slowly he tightened the cord around her neck . . .").
Above the boring sound of her own voice
she could hear him pacing back and forth overhead.
Days went by. Then he appeared, to invite them
all to the opera—Rossini, *The Barber of Seville*.
In the balcony, surrounded by shadow and music,
they didn't need words to pledge themselves to each other.
The next morning she nearly died when he told her
he was leaving—he had great troubles—
but he loved her and would come back in a year
and take her away with him, if she still loved him.
The year is up, she says. She's waiting
on this bridge for him, she knows he's in
the city, she even has an address, and she's written
a letter: "Dear Sir, Excuse me for disturbing you
about a matter you may no longer give much thought to. . . ."
She asks the young man to deliver it.
Now he's all alone on the bridge, looking down
into the greasy eddies. It's night, as always.
The lights in the neighborhood are going out,
as always. He tears the letter
into little pieces, which lift from his hand
like a quick gust of snow. The hell with her.
From now on he's going to have a good time.
It's already the next night
on a crowded, noisy street as a woman beckons

to him through a misty ice-cream-parlor window.
Suddenly he spots the girl—she's staring
at a huge bed in a department-store display.
She sees his reflection as he turns away,
pursues him, tells him she's felt all day
the strangest happiness. They pass
storefront after storefront blazoning
the paraphernalia of their dreams—fantastic
arrays of jewelry, a wedding dress of blinding
whiteness. Her gaiety enchants him.
They go to a nightclub. At first she doesn't want to,
but her mood gets the better of her. They dance
to the latest music—Wild Bill Haley's
"Thirteen Women" ("and only one man in town").
She can't stop laughing. She tells him she loves him
almost as much as—she doesn't pronounce a name.
Breathless, they step outside. A wind is rising.
A woman calls from a high window for her son.
Someone's chasing scattered newspapers.
She gives the young man a shocked look, then bolts.
He catches up with her near the bridge. Leave me!
Her voice is wild. He calls her crazy, says what she needs
is a good beating. Passersby close in, helping her
vanish. A whore approaches him. She takes his arm.
Honey, I've had my eye on you. He staggers
as she leads him to some empty coal sacks under
the bridge. He recoils. She calls for her friends.
Shadows spill out of a doorway. He fights them all.
Don't hurt him! she pleads. Somebody knocks her down.
Why am I always the one who has to suffer?
she cries. He stumbles from the melee,
blood on his shirtfront, goes back
to the bridge. The girl, halfway across, faces him.
He didn't come, she says. You were right, I was
stupid and selfish. How clear things appear to me now.
It's his turn to confess.
I tore up your letter, I was thinking only of myself,

44

I too was dreaming. Letter or no letter,
she replies, it doesn't make any difference.
They step down into a skiff and row
on the canal—through cavernous arcades,
past embankments on which trash fires
illuminate armies of the sleeping poor.
Overcome with relief, he forgets his fear.
He'll wait patiently for her to come around.
He'll get a decent job, work hard for them both.
Someday, she says, looking away. Soon, though,
they're talking about what doesn't seem very far off.
It starts to snow. Astonished,
What does it signal, they wonder, this whiteness
falling on everything? They enter a little park
overlooking the city. They horse around in the snow,
they hold each other close, start walking again.
The snow stops. It's day as they arrive
back where they set out from so many hours ago,
the square, the canal, the bridge, on which
someone dressed in black stands motionless.
Wide-eyed, she whispers, It's him!, takes a couple of
uncertain steps, then rushes into his arms.
She runs back to the young man, looks in his eyes—
is it for what she finds, or doesn't find?—
and slowly, since time doesn't matter anymore,
returns to the one who's on the bridge,
who's staring out to sea, away from the ending
that's just taken place, away from all endings.

Legends

—for Charles Simic

1.

But few, after all, can forget the old country,
its tales of witches and lycanthropy,
narrow roads that climb toward fogbound
heights whose abandoned settlements
he approaches cautiously, not sure what he will find,
as now, in a story of another kind,
he walks upstairs to an unlit second floor
and glances from the window before pulling the shade.

2.

What are the odds these days on cause and effect?
A hundred to one against, as a matter of fact,
says a diplomatic friend. But sooner or later
pattern, the smoking gun, works its way clear
of even the most chaotic scheming.
Any moment makes a joke of naming
whatever happens. The stars, for instance—
over what distances they communicate with us.

3.

Suddenly the stony underfoot chill gets serious;
it's November, rank and bitter and mysterious
in an unkempt country garden where
a measly rain is turning into snow.
I bring thumb and forefinger to my lips and whistle.
A large black dog vaults from a thicket like a missile
onto the leaf-strewn path, something still alive
and kicking in its jaws.

4.

A harpsichord is chiming in the run-down cottage
I recently acquired as a tax advantage.

The notes are thin, icy, and exact,
their mixture of audacity and wonder
reflecting a master's touch. Just as the thought
occurs to me I wrote the piece myself, the distraught
performer at the keyboard whispers,
"I feel strange," and bursts into flame.

5.

Her vehemence helps brighten the narrow shore
on which the person I've been looking for
(he looks a little bit like Graham Greene)
sits in an armchair, uncomfortably
completing another entry in the journal
he keeps of his dreams, those endless, infernal
forays into the past, which he indexes,
but not in alphabetical order.

6.

Untended memories trailing in his wake
like the agitated cloud cartoonists make
to indicate a swarm of bees, someone
or other stops to watch his breath vanish
and wonders what the present would be really
like if the world let bygones finally
be bygones with those four outdated, largely forgotten
central issues—earth, water, fire, and air.

7.

At the hour when people know more than they know
the winter dark lets fall a powdery glow
on the pines surrounding our frontier encampment.
"Mira," whispers the soothsayer in his native tongue,
"es una noche mitológica."
Suspending his account of the tactical
innovations of the Parthians,
he makes a circle in the air with his cigar.

Nearing an Airport

Blue lights spun above the squad car facing the intersection.
I don't know, said the cabbie, some kind of accident.
We paused alongside a massive brick wall of darkened
warehouses—one extinct ocean liner after another,
hundreds of lightless windows hiding tons of water.
Steam billowed from the nostrils of manhole covers.
Overhead, cables and wires flashed like Morse or tracer.
We passed the broken doors of a onetime fire station,
then a lot of used cars asleep with their eyes open.
A 747 rose slowly from behind a cluster of oil tanks.
Its coronal silhouette loomed, blinking and humming
like some splendid, pointless mechanism designed expressly
for the absolute monarch who's never outgrown his childhood.

"Waking and Sleeping" is based on the personal record of Fritz
Reck-Malleczewen (1884–1945), published in 1947 and again in
1966 as *Tagebuch eines Verzweifelten* (Goverts Verlag, Stuttgart)
and, in Paul Reubens's translation, as *Diary of a Man in Despair*
(New York, 1970), from which the italicized lines in the poem
are direct quotations.

UNIVERSITY PRESS OF NEW ENGLAND publishes books under its own imprint and is the publisher for Brandeis University Press, Brown University Press, Clark University Press, University of Connecticut, Dartmouth College, Middlebury College Press, University of New Hampshire, University of Rhode Island, Tufts University, University of Vermont, and Wesleyan University Press.

ABOUT THE AUTHOR

Jonathan Aaron is the author of *Second Sight* (1982), a winner of the National Poetry Series Open Competition. He lives in Cambridge, Massachusetts.

LIBRARY OF CONGRESS CATALOGING-IN-PUBLICATION DATA

Aaron, Jonathan.
    Corridor / Jonathan Aaron.
      p. cm. — (Wesleyan poetry)
      ISBN 0-8195-2200-7. — ISBN 0-8195-1203-6 (pbk.)
      I. Title. II. Series.
    PS3551.A7C67   1992
    811'.54—dc20   91-50807
    ∞